the taste belongs to the gods

the first taste belongs to the gods

DELTA DONOHUE

YieldingPress

The First Taste Belongs to the Gods
Published by Yielding Press
Littleton, CO

Library of Congress Control Number: 2017949378

ISBN: 978-0-9992290-0-2

TRAVEL / Essays & Travelogues

QUANTITY PURCHASES: Schools, companies, professional groups, clubs, and other organizations may qualify for special terms when ordering quantities of this title. For information, email Delta@DeltaDonohue.com.

To Jaimala

Thank you for walking alongside
For dancing ahead
For holding doors I might never have entered
This would never have happened without you
Ever grateful

Contents

Acknowledgments

THEY SAY IT TAKES A VILLAGE TO RAISE A CHILD. IT CERtainly takes one to birth a book. Here are but a few of the amazing people who linked arms with me along the way...

Astrid—Not only do you remind me to laugh, but you rock as an accountability partner. Thank you for the many phone calls and for providing a soft shoulder to land on. And HUGE thanks for holding my hand through the process of creating a logo and a brand. Your talent is as immense as your spirit.

Gayla and Rocky—Thank you for ever so gently (and occasionally forcefully) guiding me through editing and proofing. Your wisdom and objectivity brought a greater depth to this book.

My Word Publishing and Polly, Andrea and Micah P.—I found you late, but boy am I glad I did. Thank you for your expert management and helping me find my way through the jungle!

Shout out to the regulars in Erin Zimmer's Dedicated Writing Group: Erin, Jill, Carryl, Heidi, Chrome, Lisa, Josh, and Vaughn. Your constant encouragement helped keep me going, especially in those moments when I wanted to stop.

The children, women, volunteers, and staff of Vatsalya and Anoothi—Thank you for letting me step into your lives. We've laughed, cried, sung, and danced...and through it all, we have loved.

My mother, first for putting up with me during the stressful times and also for being my constant cheerleader.

My wonderful children, now adults, Micah and Miriam, my daughter-in-law, Melissa, and my unbelievably darling grandson, Elliot. Life is so much richer because of all of you.

Introduction

THE TRAJECTORY OF MY LIFE HASN'T BEEN A STRAIGHT line. Far from it! I never dreamed of working in India. I barely knew where it was on a world map.

In my late 40s, I was working in middle management for corporate America and unhappy. I knew I wanted more and that I would never find it if I stayed in my safe little life. I had a vague dream about working with women but no real idea how to bring that dream into being.

Six months later, at the age of 47, I quit my job. I spent a lot of time writing and going on long walks, trying to figure out what was next. I also started sharing my dream with everyone I knew. A good friend introduced me to Jaimala and Hitesh Gupta in India. They ran a Non-Governmental Organization (NGO) named Vatsalya. As part of their mission, they had a home for orphaned and abandoned children. While it wasn't working with women, something drew me to this opportunity. I spent several months emailing questions and thoughts back and forth before I finally committed to go to India and volunteer with the children.

My first stay was four months. During that time, I became fast friends with Jaimala and Hitesh. Jaimala and I had long talks about my desire to do something meaningful in this next chapter of my life. She was fully supportive of my desire to work with women. In fact, it was my first exposure to how Jaimala works. She is one of those "be careful what you wish for" people because she will make it happen, and quickly!

Over many cups of chai, we hatched Anoothi, a microcredit social enterprise that partners with village women. The women are supported by programming created by the NGO, receiving training in health, hygiene, and gender equality. Anoothi provides the space and resources for them to revive traditional arts such as hand-block printing and patwa (thread) jewelry-making. Jaimala is Anoothi's feet on the ground. I take the completed products and sell them in the US. The best thing about Anoothi—besides the women themselves—is that it teaches each woman a skill that can produce sustainable income. Anoothi became the fulfillment of my dream without me even realizing it!

This book of poems and stories is not your typical travelogue. Instead, it reflects my internal journey and observations as I traveled back and forth to India from 2007 to 2014. It is my hope that you will enjoy reading about those experiences and laugh a little, maybe even cry a little. It is my deeper hope that, for some (or all!) of you, this book may provide an invitation to ask of yourselves, "What is calling me? What life do I dream of?"

My choice to go to India, build a business, and return again and again has forever changed my life. As you will see in the chapters that follow, it hasn't always been easy. But it has always been worth it. Namaste!

The People

In these poems and stories, I have changed the names of all the wonderful children I met at Vatsalya, the women of Anoothi, and the staff that worked for both. I have used the real names of Jaimala and Hitesh Gupta, with their permission, as they have walked so much of this journey with me.

The Organizations

Vatsalya
Founders: Jaimala and Hitesh Gupta
vatsalya.org

Mission:
Vatsalya is a Sanskrit word meaning "unconditional motherly love." Vatsalya has undertaken projects and interventions that spread over the entire state of Rajasthan. We have a unique Children's Village on the outskirts of Jaipur where about 60 orphaned, abandoned and destitute children live under the loving care of Vatsalya's staff.

In addition, there are monthly programs that reach over 800 children in the slums. Vatsalya also works in the areas of health, HIV-AIDS prevention, and women's empowerment.

Anoothi India

Founders: Jaimala Gupta and Delta Donohue

facebook.com/anoothiindia/

Mission:

Provide high quality, focused vocational training and employment to enable marginalized women of India to enhance their standard of living, sense of dignity and independence.

Anoothi US

Founder: Delta Donohue

anoothius.com

Mission:

Anoothi US provides opportunities for women around the world to find common ground through compelling stories and unique, quality products.

The Place

Jaipur

Jaipur is the capital of the state of Rajasthan located in Northern India. It is often called the Pink City, a reference to the color of its famous city buildings. It is part of the Golden Triangle tourist circle along with New Delhi and Agra.

The Grandmother

HAVE YOU EVER NOTICED HOW THE JOURNEY BEGINS before you expect it to start? Mine started the moment I set foot on the plane from Newark to Delhi. My seat was toward the back of the plane. Almost everyone was done boarding and seated by the time I got to my seat. An elderly Indian woman was standing in the aisle a couple of rows ahead of me.

There is a certain type of Indian woman who both impresses and intimidates me: the Indian Grandmother.

Small in stature
Wire-framed glasses
Thinning grey hair
Intricately twisted into a bun
At the nape of her neck,

Sari muted in color
An ever-present cardigan or shawl
Wrapped tightly
Covering her entire body
For she is never warm enough.

I saw several of these grandmothers on my flight last night, but one in particular caught my attention. I'll call her Noni ji. I don't know if that's an actual word, but there was a five-year-old next to me going to Delhi to see his grandmother for the first time and he kept chatting excitedly about meeting his Noni. I've added the 'ji' as a sign of respect like Indians do.

She stood two rows ahead of me, speaking rapidly in Hindi. It was clear she was trying to figure out where she was supposed to sit as she held her boarding pass out for all to see. A couple of helpful passengers let her know that she had the middle seat in the center section, right where she was standing. They repeatedly pointed to the empty seat, to Noni ji, to her boarding pass, and back to the empty seat. None of this seemed to impact her in the slightest. Anyone watching could tell, without the need for translation, Noni ji didn't want to sit in the middle seat in the center section. In fact, she wanted the aisle seat—possibly any aisle seat—but there was one in the next row, at the other end, that she was definitely focused on.

Soon a United flight attendant was at her side. Welcome to United Airline's newest sitcom.

After a short introduction from helpful passengers explaining the situation, it began with the flight attendant explaining calmly, with ever-present hand gestures, and then with an increasing level of agitation, how Noni ji had to take her assigned seat and, once we were airborne, if an aisle seat was open, she was welcome to take it. This explanation occurred completely in English. Simultaneously, Noni ji was telling her own tale in Hindi, and even without hand gestures, her monologue was full of its own sense of drama and tension. To all watching, it was clear: neither side was making any headway! Finally, the exasperated flight attendant turned to a young Indian man sitting in the row with the coveted aisle seat.

She said, "She's your problem now. Take care of her."

He said, "What am I supposed to do?"

"You speak her language. Tell her what I've been saying!"

And then the flight attendant moved quickly to another location of the plane, never to be seen or heard from again.

Thankfully, the young man did speak Hindi and he began to talk to Noni ji. He spoke at length while other passengers continued to force their way around this small woman parked in the aisle. He pointed to her boarding pass and to the middle seat several times. Noni ji listened, patted him on the shoulder every few minutes, and nodded her head in that magical way only Indians do. Her eyes twinkled a bit as if she were thinking, "What a charming young man. He is trying to be so helpful." Then she promptly crawled over him, the passenger in the middle, and sat down in the aisle seat she had been staring at all along. At that moment, the man turned and saw that I was watching. He grinned sheepishly and held his hands up in surrender.

It turned out no one came forward to claim the aisle seat now firmly occupied by Noni ji. Maybe it had never been assigned, but it felt more like the Universe throwing up its hands saying, "What's the point? She's not going to move." Once airborne, the passenger in the middle seat, who still seemed a bit miffed over Noni ji unceremoniously crawling over him, picked up his items from the seat pocket and moved to the middle seat originally assigned to Noni ji. His move may have been further encouraged by how frequently Noni ji kept leaning over him to ask her helpful young man questions.

During the 13-hour flight, I had many opportunities to watch the young man continue taking care of Noni ji. He would walk around to her seat and kneel down. He helped her figure out the touch-screen TV and how to fill out her customs form. Several times through the night I saw him quietly talking with her. When we landed in Delhi and were all lined up to depart the plane, they were both right in front of me. He placed his hand on her shoulder, leaned down and spoke into her ear. I imagined he was wishing her safe travels for the rest of her journey. She looked at him for a moment, again with that twinkle in her eyes, and motioned for him to bend down again so she could speak directly to him. An instant later he was getting her carry-on luggage from the overhead bin. This consisted of a small roller bag and two large plastic bags stuffed to the brim and filled with who knows what. The last time I saw the two of them, he was still managing her bags and she was holding his arm.

The word that comes to mind when I try to describe Noni ji is "formidable." She never raised her voice, had a constant twinkle in her eyes, and always got exactly what she wanted.

What a way to start the journey!

The Drive

MY FIRST IMPRESSION, EVERY TIME I LEAVE CUSTOMS and enter the part of the Delhi airport where arriving passengers are met, is this swarming mass of humanity. Even at midnight, it's staggering.

Sanchit and Ravi pick me up at the airport. I have known each for seven years, first as awkward adolescents living at Vatsalya and now as full-fledged staff members. Poised and confident, they expertly maneuver my luggage and me through the jumble of people, luggage carts, and vendors until we finally arrive at Vatsalya's brand-spanking-new Bolero Jeep. Their pride is evident as they show it to me. The old one had been on its last leg for several years and funding had finally been finagled to purchase a new one. The seats are still covered in plastic, which makes me think of *My Big Fat Greek Wedding* and how they had plastic slipcovers for all their furniture. It would be the same with this Bolero. The plastic would stay until it was shredded from use, and only then would it be removed—a bit begrudgingly.

Sanchit and Ravi don't speak much English and I am secretly glad. After too many hours traveling with too little sleep, I am looking forward to curling up on the back seat of that brand-new Bolero. Jaimala told me she was sending pillows and heavy quilts since I am arriving during the winter season and she wanted me to be comfortable during the long drive.

The trip will take anywhere between five and seven hours. This range tells you a little bit about the traffic and possible road conditions. I'd come to understand that road conditions might mean anything from construction to an overturned vehicle or being stopped behind a group of traveling nomads with their herd of camels. This time, Jaimala had warned me that areas of the route were experiencing unusual fog, which might lengthen the trip even more.

Within 45 minutes, Sanchit, Ravi, and I have exhausted our combined knowledge of English and Hindi. It is perfect timing. We have just reached the outskirts of Delhi, so I prepare to drift away into a lovely sleep.

I pull the two heavy quilts over me and arrange the pillows. It is so cold. Fun fact: Most Indian cars don't have heaters. There is no need. And for those that do, like our brand-spankin'-new Bolero…well, it has to be below freezing, with frost on your eyebrows, for an Indian to even consider turning on the heater. I am grateful for the quilts and snuggle right under them.

I am just drifting off to sleep when the jeep hits our first ginormous (yes, I know that's not a real word, but it fits) pothole. I am slammed against the ceiling and then land on the floor in front of my seat. Jaimala had warned me that I might find the Bolero a little bumpy in the back. What she failed to explain was that the Bolero had no shock absorbers—NONE! Sanchit and Ravi can't stop apologizing and I can't stop laughing. Throughout the rest of the trip, they keep asking if I am comfortable. Given that it is impossible to avoid the potholes, there really isn't a good answer, so I just keep saying yes.

For a little while, I try to figure out a way to brace myself on the seat so that I can sleep without falling off, but it just isn't going to happen. I've taken off my shoes so I won't rip the plastic wrap, but without shoes, my sock-clad feet slip off with every baby bump we hit, which gives little hope for the monster bumps. I can either forget about sleeping and sit up, or I can keep getting bounced to the floor.

It's a strange thing about India—it almost always forces me to yield.

While my good humor remains intact, the bouncing is wreaking havoc with my bladder. On my previous trips, I had always been picked up by Ojan. There was a special place he would stop midway. He said it was the only place in the middle of the night that was safe and clean. I can't remember the name of the place and I can't remember

25

how to say "I need to use the bathroom" in Hindi. I am beginning to despise the potholes. Later, Jaimala explained to me that Sanchit and Ravi asking if I was comfortable was their way of politely asking if I needed to use the bathroom. Oh, if I had only known!

As it turns out, it is probably a good thing I can't sleep. About two hours outside of Jaipur, the fog gets worse and Ravi and I help Sanchit attempt to stay in the center of the road by calling out right and left as we search for the edge of the road. After about an hour, the fog thickens to the worst I have ever experienced. Right then, Ravi and Sanchit decide to have a discussion, perhaps just the tiniest bit of an argument, about whether low beams or high beams are the best navigation for this situation. I try inserting my opinion about low beams, but they don't particularly care. At one point, they also try no lights—which I quickly and quite loudly veto.

The worst part of the fog occurs around the Amer Fort. Built in the late 1500s, the fort was used both as a palace and a military post. Today, it draws tourists from around the world. The only way up to the fort is by jeep or elephant. Tourists are charged for either mode of transportation, so most choose elephant. Once the top is reached, a photo of you perched atop your elephant is available for just a slight additional fee.

Because of this, the roads around Amer Fort are frequently traveled by elephants and their wallah trainers. Imagine being in the densest fog you've ever driven in, traveling on a winding, one-lane mountain road, and encountering an elephant in the middle of it. There really is no way to coax an elephant to move who is quite contentedly doing nothing. Our elephant takes up just enough room that it is impossible to edge along on either side. Finally, the elephant wallah arrives (not sure where he has been, perhaps taking a chai break?) and is able to encourage his elephant to move along. I am so glad to make it safely down the other side and, eight and a half hours after leaving the airport, finally drive into Jaipur.

Now, excuse me, but where's the bathroom??!!

Lice

Second day in India
Meeting with the founder
The creator of this home
For children unwanted and alone.
In the office
Another volunteer
By my side
She's been here six months
Knows the ropes
She's not sure she
Wants to share the children
Liked it when she was the only one
For them to love.

She asks if I brought oil with me
I have no idea what this means
Oil was not listed in the volunteer handbook
Or any of the travel guides I'd read
Or on the website that I had basically memorized
And what kind of oil?
Are we talking motor oil or olive oil
And why, how is it used?
Clearly my face communicates
The confusion that I feel
She explains
Some of the children
Returning from visits to their villages
Have come
Bearing gifts
Head lice
I should be prepared
To get
Head lice.

Now
I prepared for many things
Being too cold
Too hot
Tired
Dealing with the emotional burden
Of traumatized children
Language barriers

Food difficulties
Had a Ziploc baggie full of
"What if" medications
That doctors seemed all too happy to hand out.

Don't remember thinking about
The possibility of little bugs crawling through my hair
Not once.
Now all I can think about
The scene from *The Thornbirds*
Where they chop off Maggie's long, beautiful hair
Scrub her roughly with lye
Tears stream down her face
Her scalp burns
This disturbing vision loops endlessly through my brain
As I'm told about the logistics of the home
And how my time will be spent
When suddenly
Something moves, it does
I'm sure something is moving
I can feel little legs scurrying close to my ear
Quickly I reach up to scratch and to smash
While she, by my side, just sits there and laughs.

Koi Bottne

MY FIRST SUMMER AT VATSALYA, I HELPED TEACH THE youngest class at the on-campus school. Each morning we walked the dirt path to our classroom. The room was painted in vibrant yellows and oranges. The walls were decorated with painted murals showing the English alphabet—uppercase "A," lowercase "a," and a great big red apple. Toys were packed in stacking baskets and workbooks with thick pencils were piled on low tables. Everywhere I looked there were activities to stimulate a child's interest. It was like elementary classrooms around the world.

Every day, we worked on letters and shapes, motor skills, and practicing how to be kind and friendly. All activities were conducted in Hindi and English. It was the perfect way for me to learn Hindi and these activities prepared the children to grow up able to function in an increasingly English-centric world.

Amita was a small child and very shy. She didn't live at the children's home, but came from one of the nearby villages. I wondered if I was the first white woman she had seen up close. She stayed as far away from me as she could. Even after several days had passed, her fear of me seemed just as strong.

One morning, I noticed a huge sore on her arm filled with pus. I knew from talking with staff members that this wasn't unusual. The kids would get a bite or a splinter and then scratch at it. There was no running water in most villages, let alone hot water, so children struggled with hygiene. Consequently, their sores often became badly infected.

At recess break I asked an older village boy, who came with Amita every day, to show the sore to her mother that night and ask her to wash it. When Amita came back the next day, the sore looked even worse. I saw the beginning of red streaks running up her arm.

I left the other volunteer in charge of the classroom. I gently took Amita's hand and walked outside. I knew she was scared. Her little hand trembled in mine. I didn't know enough Hindi to explain to her where we were going but I kept saying, "koi bottne," a catchall phrase in Hindi that means something like "Don't worry, everything is going to be okay."

I led Amita to the kitchen area and called for Kireet, the cook. I asked him for garum panni (hot water) and some clean cloths. Kireet spoke almost no English but, after I showed him Amita's arm, it was clear that he understood. Before he left, he took the time to kneel down in front of Amita and say something very softly to her. I didn't understand what he said but I heard him end with "koi bottne."

Amita and I waited on the concrete steps while Kireet heated the water. She continued to stare at me with wide eyes. Her hand never stopped trembling. I kept talking in a low, gentle voice and would add "koi bottne" every couple of minutes.

Kireet brought out the water. I took a rag, dipped it in the hot water, and showed Amita on my own arm what I was going to do. I did this a couple of times, then picked up a clean rag and very lightly took hold of Amita's arm. Her eyes got even wider, but she remained very still. I dipped the rag into the water and laid the hot compress on her arm. Kireet knelt by her, stroking her hair. Within a moment or two, the abscess burst and pus leaked down her arm. I took another clean rag and repeated the process. We did this for several moments until the sore looked clean and pus-free.

I applied an antibiotic cream and wrapped her arm loosely while Kireet cleaned up the mess that we had made. I gathered Amita in my arms and sang *You Are My Sunshine* to her. We sang this song every day in class and I hoped it would provide some comfort. When the song was over, I set her down and stood up. She immediately put her hand in mine and started leading me back toward the classroom.

I'd like to write that Amita warmed up to the white

teacher and all of her fear melted away. I really don't know. She remained a shy little girl who continued to come to class. But the sore on her arm completely healed and that was enough.

Scolded

Oh, oh, oh,
I'm not going to listen to this
I'm not a child
My way is good enough!
She's just
Old and stubborn
Set in her ways
It's   just   a   song!
A song
We need to teach
To the children
My letters
The ones I wrote
Are good
Enough

Why does she care
That my vowels aren't written
Like they taught in
Grammar school
This is how I write now
I don't even remember
How to write
The way that she says
I am supposed to.

She does verse one
I do verse two
I look at hers
And, yes,
It looks like it
Could come out of a
Handwriting book
Plump, round letters
All exact in size
Sit proudly on lines
That are straight and even
And yes,
Mine do look a bit
Like chicken scratching
And perhaps
They aren't sitting
Quite so proudly
On lines that are a bit

Uneven and ragged
But the children
Will be able to
Read them
And that is all that matters.

We came to this home
Within days of each other
I am 48 and she,
Almost 30 years older
We stay with the older girls
She rises before the sun
Grabs shawl and flashlight
And goes to an empty room
To meditate in solitude
There is so much
Of her
That I admire
That I want to be like
Imagine
Volunteering in India
At 75
Committed, unafraid
Why does she
Have to be so concerned
With how I shape
My e's or the height of
My letters?

The two song verses
On separate pages
Are now taped to the wall
Of the classroom
She has come back over
And I see her looking
At my page
She doesn't say anything
But disapproval is
Apparent on her face
As she walks away
It's hard to capture
All of the ungracious
Thoughts running rampant
In my head
Who does she think she is?
She is just another volunteer
Like me.

I want to continue
In the pleasure
And ceaseless momentum
Of my internal whining
When I remember
Sitting with her
The first day
In the sunlight

She talked
About the joy
Of being a mentor
The opportunity
To be with these children
To share, to shape
To listen, to learn.

On a clean piece of paper
I begin again
And laboriously
Try to create
Exactly spaced
Fat round letters
That perch
Proudly
On straight, even lines
Wanting to give
The best that I can.

Anoothi—The Beginning

Fifteen of us
In the desert
The sun greets the sky
Already the day warms
We choose
To sit outside
A dirt courtyard
Spreading rugs
In circle
We work
Beads and stones
Stringing geometric patterns
Into beauty
I will take back
To my land
To sell.

As each piece is finished, it is passed around the circle and I clap enthusiastically while the village women look at me with shock and a bemused tolerance. Occasionally, they have a design question and the entire group becomes animated with debate. There is always a moment, however, when I notice they want me to make the final decision.

It is not my decision to make.

> *But we don't know.*

These are your designs. Do you like them?

> *Yes.*

Are they well made?

> *Of course!* (This said with a great sense of group pride and almost disgust that the question was asked.)

Do you feel good about them?

> *Yes, but we don't know if they will sell.*

Neither do I. This is our first attempt. All we can do is learn from what sells and adjust.

> *Please*

Even though
That word is never uttered
The longing is clear
Tell us what to do
Make the decision
Take the responsibility
After all
This was your idea.

And it was, in the beginning. I was here with a dream. I wanted to build a relationship with these women and learn and share their stories in the hopes of building bridges and breaking barriers. The jewelry was a way to bring needed income. We had talked about many options and this was the one that the women thought was the best. It required the least amount of start-up capital and Jaipur is one of the world's centers for semi-precious stones. It seemed to make the most sense even though none of us had any ex-perience designing or making jewelry. All along the way, at every major decision point, the women had been involved. This organization was built on the concept of partnership. It wasn't mine, it wasn't Jaimala's, and it wasn't the women's. It was all of ours. Yet, now, they are demanding I make the decisions.

And so
Silence lingers
And lingers
The awkward pause
Necessary
Creating space
For those unused to
Giving voice
To opinions
Risking the
Leap of creative choice.

And then, because life is not simple, just after I determine not to voice my opinion or make the decision, we come to the place where I not only voice my opinion but firmly put my foot down. Quality Control. Not a concept they are familiar with, at least in this context, nor one they have any desire to become familiar with! The conversation goes something like this:

No, it's not okay to send it this way!

It looks fine. What's next?

It's not fine. You have five beads on this side and four on the other side.

It looks fine.

It needs to be the same on both sides or it won't sell.

It looks fine. What's next?

Wait, this bracelet, all of the stones are black but there is a small pink one here.

It looks fine.

It needs to be all black stones—or you could put in a large pink stone—call attention to it.

It looks fine! BAS! (a Hindi word, here sounding quite like I am being sworn at, meaning "Enough!")

We go around and around. Most of the time, the jewelry ends up getting re-made. Although, occasionally, out of sheer exhaustion, I give up and take a necklace with five beads on one side and four on the other, or a shining black onyx bracelet with a lonely pink pearl thrown in, wondering how in the world I will sell them.

The Auntie

EACH TIME I CAME TO INDIA, VOLUNTEERED AT
Vatsalya, and worked with the Anoothi women, I found myself stretched, taken to points beyond my comfort zone. I
welcomed the introduction of new friendships and the unexpected encounters with those just met, who entered my
world as if I had known them my entire life.

I met Padmal on my first visit. She was an "Auntie" who
lived full-time on the campus, acting as one of the resident
house-moms caring for the younger children and doing
whatever else needed to be done. I had read the descrip-
tion of house-moms and realized the incredible amount of
work they did, but somehow I passed over the true meaning of the title. I just assumed they were a bit like the camp
counselors I experienced when, at 12 years old, I went to
summer camp and slept away from home at Camp Chief

Ouray. Counselors who wanted the job experience, did what needed to be done, kept all of their charges reasonably intact, but didn't deeply care about the children. This was the expectation that I ignorantly brought with me to Vatsalya.

I could not have been more wrong. There were several Aunties at Vatsalya. Most lived on-campus, although there were a few that traveled back and forth from nearby villages. What united all of them was a deep love for the children and a commitment to raise them with care, as if they were their own. They were mothers in the truest and most complete sense of the word. Mothers committed to the 70 children who lived at Vatsalya. It is largely due to them that Vatsalya was a real home, and not just a residential care center.

Padmal captured my heart. I didn't expect that to happen. She seemed a bit gruff originally, even though she had a smile that lit up her entire face. My first memory of her was when she came into the older girls' unit to clean. I tried to take the twig broom from her to let her know that I would do it and she slapped my hand, not harshly but decisively, letting me know that she was there to do a job and I darn well better let her do it. Later, I would watch her use that same broom to go after a mouse that had dared to enter one of her units. She was undaunted by the speed of the mouse and there was no question who was going to be the victor. The mouse was quickly swept out of the unit and hopefully found a place to reside out of Padmal's reach.

There are several memories of her with the children and the amazing care she provided each of them. She was firm but fair and loving. Throughout my stays there, time and time again, I saw little ones run to her for a hug or for help with whatever was disturbing their day. No matter how busy she was, she always made time for them. She was also quick to remind them about chores and to reprimand anyone who was behaving inappropriately or who'd managed to forget some daily obligation.

This "anyone" could include foreign volunteers, as I was soon to learn. One day I was walking on the path and Padmal was out hanging laundry. I went up to her to say hello and she stared at me with an odd look on her face. She grabbed my face with hands that demonstrated the strength of a lifetime of hard work. She turned my head to the side. Soon she was yelling for one of the little children while still holding my head in her vise-like grip. I didn't have any idea what was going on but I knew she was leading me, and my head, to one of the concrete benches and suddenly I was sitting, still firmly held in her iron grasp.

The little child reappeared with what seemed to be wooden matches in his hand. I was beginning to get a little bit nervous now. Padmal took one of the wooden matchsticks and roughly turned my head so that my left ear was basically touching my left shoulder. She began to clean out my right ear with the matchstick. Apparently in my cold-water bucket showers, I had not paid sufficient attention to ear hygiene and Padmal wasn't going to allow that! I was equal parts appalled and humiliated but she didn't even notice. There was nothing to be done but to sit there and internally vow to pay much better attention during my bucket showers in the future! Should I remind everyone that I was 48 years old at the time? It didn't matter. As long as I was on the campus, it meant I was in her care and a dirty ear was just not going to be tolerated.

Not long into my stay, I had a phone call with my mom back in the United States. She told me that her sister, my aunt, had passed away. I found myself feeling very homesick. I went into my unit, sat on my bed, and began to cry. Part of me really felt I should go home and be with my mother. Padmal came in. I'm not sure why. Perhaps she had seen me and just knew that I needed someone. She sat next to me on the bed. She spoke very limited English and I spoke even more limited Hindi. Yet somehow, we managed to communicate.

I knew the Hindi words for mom and sister, but I didn't know how to communicate someone dying. I looked at Padmal after saying my mom's sister and raising my hand to the ceiling, trying somehow to communicate leaving this world, or death, or heaven, or...

Padmal looked at me for a few moments and tears began to form in her eyes. She reached over and gave me a hug, a hard hug. This wasn't a woman who hugged easily or often. Her hug felt like being embraced by a lumberjack who swung an ax every day of his life. I looked at her and she began to talk using a combination of simple Hindi, awkward English, and sign language. I came to understand that she and I were the same age and she had had ten children. Seven of those children had died.

It took me several moments and many questions back and forth before I believed that I really did understand what she was saying. Seven of her children had died. I don't know how or when. My Hindi and her sign language didn't take us that far. What I do know is that we sat in silence, holding hands, grieving for those we loved who had left us.

I didn't know Padmal well, or much of her story, but I did know this—by the end of my stay, I considered her my friend.

Right of Way

I start with a simple fact
The pedestrian has no standing
In the midst of the bedlam
That is the traffic of India

At first everything seems jumbled and harried
This place where striped lanes and stoplights
Provide the merest hint of suggestion
In the best of times
Even so
After studying
A pattern begins to emerge
In the din of never-ending horns.

There is a hierarchy of sorts
Determined by size
Trucks and buses rule because
Well, think about it,
They can smash everything else.
Oh, but wait, there is an exception
I forgot. I should start with the cow.
Nothing trumps the cow.
Aside from that
Trucks and buses
Definitely rule.
In a battle between trucks,
Which happens frequently,
The truck whose horn lasts longest
With the most pitches—wins
After trucks and buses
We move to cars
Although sometimes it seems
That donkeys or camels pulling carts
Take precedence.
Then auto rickshaws
Otherwise known as tuk-tuks
Bicycles
Finally human rickshaws
You might notice
I fail to mention
Motorcycles
Because they don't count

THE FIRST TASTE BELONGS TO THE GODS

They simply swerve in and out
Obeying no rules or rhythm
But watching motorcycles
Always makes me think of that comedy bit
You know the one
How many people can fit into a VW bug?
In India, it's a daily occurrence,
Not just with cars but motorcycles also
Not uncommon to see a family of six
Now it's true
Many Indians are quite thin
So, assuming you have a dad that's thin
Three small children
And the baby, he's in the mother's arms of course,
And she is very thin
Despite having given birth to four children
Add them up
Six humans
One motorcycle
I don't quite understand how it is possible.
It helps that no space is taken up by helmets.
But back to the hierarchy
I left off at human rickshaws
Which then takes us to the pedestrian

Before I address the pedestrian
I should mention the elephant
There aren't many in the cities

More of a tourist thing these days
But occasionally you'll turn a corner
And there will be an elephant
Just standing there
You have to wonder
If the big guy is a little lost
Or dreaming of a jungle.
Easy to guess who gets
Right of way
Doesn't seem to matter if
Truck, bus, bike, or tuk-tuk
Or even cow, because the cows just ignore
The gigantic grey thing in the center of the road
But for everyone and everything else
I mean it's an elephant
What are you going to do?

That question though
What are you going to do?
Is not one to pose to an Indian driver
For there is always something to do
It may mean teetering on two wheels
Along the banks of a ditch
Driving the wrong way into oncoming traffic
Or creating a road
On the dirt in front of village shops
And yes, sometimes, oh so occasionally, it means
Waiting for the elephant to pass.

There is one unwritten traffic rule
Observed by all
No honking at an elephant.

Back to the lowly pedestrian
Picture one white foreigner
Coming from a land where motorists actually slow down
And stop to let you pass
This white foreigner
Might just happen to be a woman around 53 years of age
Simply trying
To get from one side of the street to the other
While in the back of her mind
A disconcerting bit of knowledge rumbles
Aware of a law
Learned by happenstance
Indian truck drivers can hit and kill
Six pedestrians before they go to jail
Yes, take a moment
Let that sink into the very fiber of your being
As this 53-year-old white woman is dashing between
Camels, tuk-tuks,
Swerving motorbikes, trucks and cars
All with horns blaring
Well, not the camels,
There should have been an elephant
It would have made the story better
And the crossing easier

But yes, it is true.
In a land of one billion people
Where most roads are not graced
By any type of light
The battle of truck versus person
Occurs with such regularity
It has lost all meaning
The government figures
The odds are against the drivers
Unrealistic to think
They can avoid hitting everyone
Progress though
A new law
Each truck contains a spotter
A person to help spot things
To avoid—like—people!
You get six free, but on the seventh
Off to jail
I should go back to where I started though
Hit one cow
It's a one-way ticket
Directly to jail
No passing go, throw away the key
Welcome to the traffic that is India.

Unexpected Lessons

HAVE YOU EVER BEEN UNEXPECTEDLY SCHOOLED BY someone? Taken to task? Called to the principal's office? This happens frequently to me in India—sometimes gentle, sometimes harsh pricks beneath my skin, forcing me to pause and consider.

Two stories, neither one of which I fully understand.

It was a month and a half into my first stay at Vatsalya. Three of us had gone in the jeep to the village to buy fresh produce. We bought everything on the list and were getting ready to return to the campus when the staff member remembered he needed to get one more thing, leaving Angela, a German volunteer, and me sitting in the front seat of the jeep.

Enter the midget cow. She was standing perhaps 30 or 40 feet ahead in the center of the dirt road, contentedly munching on something. A midget cow—full-size body on short, stumpy legs. Angela and I began to make fun of her because, well, really, she looked ridiculous. Suddenly, she stopped chewing, turned and looked directly at us. We both stopped laughing instantly. It was clear, without any question, she was looking right at us.

The midget cow began to walk over to us and before we knew it, her head was stretching through the window of the jeep until her nose was inches from my own. She turned her head slightly as if to say, "Really? Really! You are going to make fun of me?"

Angela and I simultaneously blurted out, "I'm sorry!" The midget cow blinked once, gave us one more long stare with those dark, soulful eyes, then backed her head out of the jeep and walked away.

I don't know what I think about animals being sentient beings, which means more than just the ability to feel, it means they perceive. And don't even get me started on how a midget cow was suddenly tall enough to reach into the window of a jeep! But it happened, ask Angela! What I do know, without any question, is: I had just been schooled by a midget cow and I have done my best, ever since, to never mock another animal.

The second story isn't exactly about being schooled. If I'm being completely honest, I'm not sure what it's about, but I know there are lessons here and so I continue to pay attention.

Jaimala and I were meeting with a new group of village women to try and interest them in Anoothi. It's important to understand that arranging a meeting with village women in India is nothing like setting up a meeting in the States. It takes days of pre-meetings and communications involving trips over bumpy roads, long dusty walks, meetings with village elders (who, of course, are always men) to obtain their permission for us to meet with the women, and then, once we've gotten their permission, multiple trips, again over bumpy roads followed by long dusty walks, to arrange a time that everyone agrees to. Usually this process happens four or five times before we come to agreement on a date and time. Business in India, at least in villages, requires a great deal of patience.

Finally, the meeting was set. Jaimala and I were in the dirt courtyard of a group of six houses made of mud plaster. Twenty women were all seated in a circle on the ground. Their children played in the dirt nearby and were blatantly curious about the presence of the white woman. Occasionally, one or two were brave enough, and curious enough, to creep close and stare at my face before running away. Always a spectacle in this environment. No way to blend in.

Before I get to the next part of the story, I have to tell you about the ants in India. I have encountered four types; three are fairly innocent. There is the small ant—very similar to America's sugar ant. I would take an early walk each morning at Vatsalya and see Ram Kumar ji, one of the teachers and a devout Hindu, using a soft straw brush to sweep the ants off the footpath so that no one would step on them—such reverence for all living things.

Then there were regular-size black ants and regular-size red ants. Both very similar to ones you would find in the United States. They pretty much leave you alone unless you harass them.

The last ant, however, I have named the Monster Ant. It is easily an inch and a half long with three well-defined body parts. Think of an ant on steroids! The hind part lifts up in the air like a scorpion's tail. Their bite was deep, extremely painful, and frequently led to infection. I did my best to stay well clear of the Monster Ant.

So, there we were, sitting in a circle. Jaimala begins speaking in Hindi, and within moments has the entire group of women, and many of the children, completely captivated. Understand: first, she is Brahmin—the highest caste—and there she is sitting in the dirt with them, ignoring the chair they offered, drinking chai from their pottery, which is still almost unheard of even though the caste system is technically illegal. And then, there is Jaimala's ability to weave a tale. I only understood a few of the Hindi words, but I knew she had them in her storytelling spell. I could tell by the heads bobbing together and the tongues clicking together—a sign of sympathy, regret, or deep understanding.

I was watching all of this when I looked down and saw a Monster Ant on my arm. I am not good with bugs. I am especially not good with the type that can hurt you badly.

We had worked so hard to set up this meeting and it was going so well. I just couldn't disrupt the meeting. Trying not to panic, I remembered Ram Kumar ji gently sweeping the ants out of harm's way. I began an instant, internal dialogue with Mr. Ant. Notice I removed the monster part—that just no longer seemed polite as I was trying to establish communication and a relationship.

Dear Mr. Ant. Hi. I'm a little bit afraid of you, but I am going to trust that you are just very, very curious and you mean me no harm. I give you my word I will not harm you. I am going to just sit here and breathe as I listen to the story and I am going to let you go on your way. I would really appreciate it if you didn't bite me.

I am being completely honest when I tell you I was having this conversation with Mr. Ant in my head and was desperately hoping it would work. I repeated it over and over and tried to listen to Jaimala but mostly followed the progress of Mr. Ant as he walked up my arm, down my back, up my back, across my bra strap and then finally down my other arm, down my fingers, and on to the dirt. I was so proud. I felt completely connected with life. Zinging with all the shared energy of the Universe. Amazing!

Of course it doesn't end there.

The ant walked in front of Jaimala. The village woman sitting next to her saw it, picked it up, squished it, and threw it behind her. My little bubble of happiness burst just a bit.

The lessons. This is what I have learned so far:

It's important to revere life.

I can stay calm in moments where I would normally panic.

Perhaps talking to animals and ants makes a difference.

And maybe, just maybe, if something is going to harm you, or your guest, particularly if your guest is Brahmin, it might just be okay to squish it. But I'm a little iffy on that one.

Shruthi

THREE MONTHS LIVING IN THIS VILLAGE FOR CHILDREN who needed a place to live and be loved. Most were orphans but some had parents that couldn't afford to take care of them, or didn't want to.

I lived in the older girls' residence. Ten teenage girls. Enough said, right?!

Actually, it was easy with all of the girls except one, Shruthi, who was probably around 16. It's hard to tell an exact age when you don't have a birth certificate. Shruthi had this way of letting me know that I was invading her space and her life would be a whole lot better the moment I left. There is nothing quite like the icy stare of a 16-year-old girl. I tried everything I could think of to win her over but it didn't work. I had to just let it go.

The holiday of Diwali was approaching. It's a huge Hindu holiday, the Festival of Lights, and it lasts for five incredible days. It's a little bit like Christmas on steroids. Families go all out, and homes, streets, and markets are decorated with beautiful hanging lights. For the kids that still had parents, this was a chance to go home, as long as it was safe, and celebrate with their families.

The families of some of Vatsalya's children lived in one of the largest slums in Jaipur. Shruthi and her sister were two of those children. Her mother and an older brother lived in the slum. I was invited to go along as we drove them home.

I stepped out of the car into layers of smells so intense my eyes burned and tears unwillingly crept down my cheeks. Trash heaps taller than me created a border between the city and the slum. Pigs and dogs roamed happily, digging for scraps. We followed a narrow footpath through this maze as people came out of their shacks to stare at the white woman. We were a tight little line—a staff member from Vatsalya, Shruthi, her sister, and then me.

We had only gone a short way when Shruthi yelled for us to stop and came back to me. She yanked my backpack off and checked to make sure that all of the snaps and buckles were fastened. She handed the backpack to me and told the staff member to keep going. She stayed behind me and walked almost right up against me. I mean almost touching me, she was that close. Protecting me. I don't know from what, and wasn't sure I wanted to know. This was her neighborhood, her world, and she was taking care of me.

We got to her one-room shack: corrugated metal roof, mud plaster walls, a dirt floor. We were invited inside and Shruthi's mother eagerly offered us chai. Her brother started showing us the electrical cord he had brought in through a hole in the corner. It was very clear that the local electric company was not aware of this arrangement. The cord snaked up the wall to a TV hanging precariously. I learned that almost all of the dwellings had television. No running water, no indoor toilets, but a TV. I didn't have any idea how to process this. As I listened, I kept thinking how this one-room shack served as kitchen, living room, and bedroom, and would sleep four people that night.

All too soon it was time to go and everyone walked us out. Again, Shruthi walked right behind me, never talking, just keeping me on the path and safe. We waved our good-byes and drove away.

Diwali passed and life returned to normal. A couple of days later, I was doing Band-Aid brigade outside the girls' residence. Mickey Mouse was the clear favorite, followed by SpongeBob SquarePants, with the lowly plain beige version falling a distant third. Suddenly, the children began to yell and I heard Shruthi's name in the Hindi chatter. I looked up and there she was walking down the pathway. Shruthi ran up to me and gave me a huge hug. The girl with the icy stare gave me a huge hug. She looked at me and said, "Did you like my home?"

Did you like my home?

I wish you could have seen her face. Shining, happy, expectant. She was thrilled that I had visited her home in the slums and met her mom and brother. She was so proud, but in her eyes, I could also see this desperate need for acceptance, for validation. She wanted me to see her family and home through her eyes.

I knew that home had nothing to do with a physical structure or an address. That it didn't matter whether it was one room or many, mud walls or marble countertops. That it had nothing to do with brick and mortar. I knew all of that. But seeing her face, feeling her joy, helped me translate that knowledge into understanding in a way that I have never felt before. I have heard that true knowledge has to live in your bones, in your muscles. This is how I felt as I looked at her beautiful face—that this true knowledge was rumbling around inside of me—changing me. There is a trite saying: Home is about heart. It was no longer trite for me. It was real and standing directly in front of me and I was grateful. This is why I was in India.

Blood Feud

The sun begins to sleep
As the family gathers
Lured by coriander and cumin
Steaming daal and
Never-ending piles of chapatti
On tables that hug the ground.
So different from
Dinners of my childhood
Where words went missing
Swallowed by whatever TV show
Eclipsed the conversation of our lives.
Here a time of noise and movement
Thunderous exclamations and gestures
By hands moist from bites just eaten
Facts and fiction fly

There is

An expectation

Beyond invitation

To participate

Even the little ones

Pose positions easily

Convictions steeped with bravado

Surpass the smallness of their frames.

Tonight

World affairs

Pakistan and India

Hindus, Muslims

References to Gandhi

Gandhi ji

Gandhi ji

His name

Spoken with a deference that is tangible

And makes me want to weep.

But within moments

The air has changed

And verbs of destruction

Rocket across the table

Until he

Slams his hand on the table

Shouting

All Muslims must die!

This is it,

This is all!

Then leans back
Against the wall
Content
As sauces
Thrown from toppled bowls
Hit the floor
Drop by drop
A slow motion explosion
In a room silenced
By the unexpected
Which lasts
But a long moment
And then
The topic changes
And new ideas
Are batted back and forth
But without me
My voice scalded by
Surprise
Vehemence
Isolated
In this room, once friends
I sit now among strangers
Identities honed
By generations of blood
That have left the ground
And nestled in the soul.

Thanksgiving

I AM UNAWARE OF DAYS PASSING. THERE IS NO CALEN-
dar to check. My only concern is remembering when I
fly back home, but that is weeks away. It was the first of
October when I arrived, so I am surprised when Jaimala
asks if I want to celebrate American Thanksgiving with the
children at Vatsalya.

It is only a week away so we immediately begin planning. My first thought is the meal! Jaimala wants complete
details. I start describing what our American dinner would
be like, aware that suddenly my answers represent an
entire country! Ah, the pressure. I figure it's best to stay
with the traditional and not mention the times my family
has opted to go with a Mexican or Italian theme just to do
something different.

The standards:

    Turkey

    Mashed potatoes and gravy

    Stuffing

    Green bean casserole

    Cranberries

    Rolls

    Sometimes a green salad

    Relish bowls of pickles and olives

        (for reasons that I've never understood!)

    And last, but not least,

    Pumpkin pie!

Hmm. There are some immediate difficulties. Turkey is out of the question on this vegetarian campus. I leave this one in Jaimala's hands, expecting that it will somehow turn into a version of daal (lentil stew). I've never seen an Indian dinner without daal. I admit that it is kind of nice to not worry about having to handle the giblets—and what exactly does one do with the neck?

We agree that mashed potatoes can be done and have never been experienced by the children. Potatoes are common, but are typically cubed and served with other roasted vegetables. I can only imagine what kind of gravy they will come up with. The only thing I'm sure of is that it will be spicy and will not contain little bits of turkey!

Stuffing prompts quite a bit of discussion. Jaimala is adamant it should be included even though I vote against it, as we aren't stuffing anything! She likes the idea of bread-crumbs and celery in some sort of dish. She again takes ownership of this item and makes notes to discuss with the head cook.

I begin to describe the green bean casserole, aware that my use of Campbell's Cream of Mushroom soup and French's Crispy Fried Onions is going to provoke certain looks of disdain if not downright audible snorts. I have never seen canned food in an Indian kitchen and certainly not something as processed as Crispy Fried Onions! After being peppered with questions about what ingredients are in the soup, we jointly devise a recipe that will include green beans grown on the campus, covered with a mush-room sauce and topped with fried onion strips. This raises another issue. There is only one oven on the campus, the one in the bakery. It will be needed for rolls and whatever pumpkin dessert we come up with. I suspect that the green bean casserole may be further adapted into a stovetop, or burner top, version.

I probably should explain how meals are made at Vatsalya. There is a large skillet, which is almost flat, used to cook roti or chapatti, the tortilla-like starch that accom-panies every meal, and two enormous pots that are cooked over burners powered by kerosene. Please understand that by enormous, I mean industrial-sized gigantic. Picture an old battered pot that can hold enough daal to feed be-tween 75–100 people.

Beyond these kerosene-powered options, there is also the solar cooker, which was a long-awaited addition to the campus. The anticipation was created not only because of a desire to increase the use of sustainable energy, but also because kerosene is expensive. There have been times when the kerosene ran out and there wasn't money to purchase more. Then the children would be served cold meals, which is very much against an Indian's nature and is contrary to the Ayurvedic teachings utilized on the campus.

Back to the Thanksgiving dinner.

As I start thinking through what we have already discussed, I'm worried about the stuffing. It sounds like it may end up being boiled breadcrumbs, apples, and celery! But, again, it's out of my hands— a statement I could use to describe the majority of my time in India.

I decide it is best to leave cranberries out of the discussion because I've never seen any in India and so I just explain that a salad would be a great addition. We opt for a traditional Indian salad of garbanzo beans, cucumbers, tomatoes, and red onions. Jaimala is relieved that at least one dish won't require any cooking.

We also decide that we can make all of the rolls a day ahead in the bakery. There isn't anything special about the rolls and it is nice to have a couple of menu items that don't require any extra work or thought!

I explain that we have relish dishes on the table with pickles and olives. She loves this because that's common at Indian tables as well. She will have bowls of pickles distributed. She then looks at me with this impish little grin and I know what she is thinking. She is remembering my first experience with Indian pickles!

We were eating dinner at her house. I think it was the first time I had been invited into her home and I was honored. By this time in India, I recognized most of the food on the table except for this small bowl that had some "blobs" in a thick sauce. I asked her what it was and she explained they were pickles! I LOVE pickles so I excitedly took one out of the sauce and popped the whole thing into my mouth just as Jaimala was actually yelling at me to stop. I couldn't imagine what was wrong. I mean a pickle is a pickle is a pickle...right? Oh my GOD! My mouth was on fire. This wasn't a pickle. This was some devilish thing invented in hell! I didn't want to be rude and spit it out but I couldn't finish chewing it and it was too big to just swallow. Tears were now streaming down my face and Jaimala was also crying—but not because her mouth was burning off her face. She was crying because she was laughing so hard. I finally did the unthinkable and spit it out into my nice cloth napkin, making the decision that offending Jaimala was preferable to choking to death while burning holes in my esophagus. Once we both stopped crying, we came to a cross-cultural agreement that I was allowed to ignore pickles and it would not be seen as rude by my host.

The last item to be planned for Thanksgiving is pumpkin pie. I've not seen a pumpkin in India but Jaimala assures me they can get them. We won't have pies exactly, as they don't have any pie pans and it would be too great an expense to purchase. But it is important to have dessert. Not only is it Thanksgiving tradition, it's also a holiday, and sweets always accompany holiday celebrations in India. I've never met an Indian who doesn't love sweets and Jaimala is no exception. She decides that she is going to create the recipe for this special treat herself.

The dinner is planned!

Now for the festivities. The evenings are cool but not cold yet. We decide that the children and staff will build the framework for a bonfire, and I can tell the story of the American Thanksgiving with Jaimala translating in front of a blazing fire. I am grateful that we are planning this a couple of days ahead. I want to reach out to my friend Google and make sure that I remember all of the important parts. Again, I feel this strange sense of national responsibility. After all, I'm educating 72 children and assorted staff members about an important part of America's history. It seems important that I get it right.

Finally, the day arrives. The campus is abuzz! The cooks and helpers are busy making the feast. The children are busy cleaning the campus and finding any spare wood or trash for the bonfire. Sacred chalk designs line the dirt pathway as is typical in Indian celebrations. A very light lunch was served so that everyone can gorge on this special dinner.

The meal is a success—although I'm not sure that it bears any resemblance to an American Thanksgiving meal. It looks and tastes very much like, well, an Indian meal. The kids are delighted to have rolls with dinner as that is unusual and like every holiday meal, there are more dishes than normal. Jaimala's pumpkin sweet is a huge success. It looks like a mini-dumpling with a sweet filling inside. If I didn't know that it was pumpkin, I probably would guess that it was a spiced apple tart. But, the kids and staff love it and that really is all that matters.

The sky begins to grow dark and it is time to light the bonfire. Children and staff gather in a circle around the fire. The heat is so intense that shawls, sweaters, and blankets are quickly set aside. Finally, it is time for the story. Jaimala and I sit side by side on a blanket. After a moment or two, we are in perfect sync. I start with the Pilgrims leaving England and an oppressive king who dictated how God should be worshipped. Jaimala seems to know the moment I am going to stop. She begins in quiet Hindi building into moments where even I can feel the tension of the journey. I liberally embellish—adding details that I think the children will enjoy and that might have been possible. After all, in an ocean-crossing journey there would be creaking ships, frightful storms, and heroics around every corner. I secretly suspect that Jaimala does her own bit of embellishment. But regardless, the children are enthralled, particularly when we describe the relationship with the American Indians and how those Native Americans helped the settlers during the harsh winter. Together we paint quite the picture of how they all came together to celebrate around a harvest table.

When the story is done, everyone cheers "Wah! Wah! Wah!" We answer a few questions and then the group settles into a cozy silence watching the bonfire burn until only embers remain. The Aunties, ever the caretakers, gather the sleepy children and take them to their rooms and the staff retires to theirs. The first American Thanksgiving at Vatsalya has come to an end.

Fear

Dubbed
The three sisters
We traveled
A luxury hotel
Framed by the Himalayas
Peaks shrouded in clouds
Five days
Dedicated
To learning
The art
Of being appreciative
The day's agenda finished
A decision
Visit the Monkey Temple
Beautiful, late afternoon sun

Encouraged the walk

Our route

More circuitous than anticipated

Dusk loomed as

We approached steps

Cut into stone

Ivy covered walls

Foliage, thick and lush,

Arched overhead

Here and there

Daring and brazen

Monkeys darted

We continued to climb

Foliage brushed our faces

Hiding the sun

Until, at last,

The temple

We separated

To explore

To pause

I hold no memory of shrines

Instead I remember

The dogs

That roamed

Emaciated

Each rib in sharp relief

Heads down

To scavenge
In hopes of a missed morsel
Except
When a person crossed their path
Then heads would raise
Not just the one
The entire pack
And eyes would lock
Teeth would bare
And growls
Guttural and piercing
Froze any movement
And prompted a quick retreat

I began to search for my companions
To discover
As the sky had darkened
Others had left
Now only three of us
The ever-present monkeys
Howling and hooting
The pack of dogs
Circling
Hunting for sustenance
And a group of young men
Circled around a fire
Watching us
With the same intensity
As the dogs

We moved into a corner
She said
I don't feel safe
As I said
We need to leave
We turned to our Indian friend
And asked
Her thoughts
Perhaps we were
Being silly foreigners
She responded
It is dark here
We must leave
Now
This darkness
Had nothing to do
With the absence of the sun.
Without speaking
We grabbed each other's hands
And began the descent
Branches scraped our faces
And monkeys taunted us
With their cries
Reaching for our hair and clothes
As we scrambled down
Endless stairs
Until we emerged into the courtyard
And walked until

THE FIRST TASTE BELONGS TO THE GODS

We found a car
To take us back to the hotel
In all of my travels
It is the only time
I felt fear.

Two Lies and a Truth

THERE IS A GAME CALLED TWO TRUTHS AND A LIE. IT'S one of those icebreaker games for groups. You invent one lie about your life and think of two truths and try to have the group guess which is the lie. This is kind of the opposite. I'll start with a lie. But let me explain the setting first.

Being an American in India wasn't always an easy thing. My first trip to India was in 2008—right at the end of George W. Bush's presidency. Bush Senior was well-respected in India and the Clintons were adored, but the same couldn't be said for George W. Regardless of where I stood politically, it was a fact that the majority of Indians I met didn't hold Americans in high esteem, largely because of the image projected by Bush post-9/11. As a foreigner, I was often put in the position of defending my country and my nation's policies. I got tired of being asked about Bush and his shock-and-awe campaigns, and what did he really mean by Axis of Evil? Time and time again, we would have discussions about his being a cowboy and how rash his actions were.

Reactions were strong enough that I began to lie and tell people that I was from Canada. After all, everyone loves Canadians.

I'll insert the truth here. I am a typical American, and by that, I mean a typical ignorant American. I'm not proud of this but it is true and especially evident when I am traveling. I know just enough about politics to be dangerous but certainly not enough to try to accurately describe our policies. Educated Indians are well aware of domestic and international politics and love to spend time discussing and debating world affairs. There were many times when I was acutely embarrassed by my lack of knowledge about current affairs—and don't get me started about geography. At least now I knew where India was!

My ignorance of world affairs made it even easier to utilize the Canadian lie. No one ever asked me about Canada's policies. The only thing that ever came up was how much better a country Canada was than the United States. I would usually choose to remain silent when this type of comment was made. If I were traveling today and continuing my lie of Canadian citizenship, I would need to become well-versed in Canadian policies, as PM Trudeau has made such a positive impression around the world!

The other situation where I routinely lied in India dealt with being single. A woman traveling alone is unusual. A woman in her late 40s or early 50s traveling alone is unheard of, particularly in the villages. Everywhere I went, I was asked about my marital status. They asked how my husband could possibly let me travel alone. Surely, he was joining me shortly. Initially I told everyone the truth—I was divorced. But this just seemed to provoke great confusion. The divorce rate, while growing, remains very low in India. During my travels it was about three out of 1,000—compared to America's 500 out of 1,000.

When I would visit a new village to try and interest them in Anoothi, the women would ask, "Where is your husband? When is he joining you?"

Explaining that I divorced several years ago and remained single largely by choice just created blank stares. It was as if there were no context within which they could process this information.

I finally found a cheap imitation wedding ring and began wearing it. If I was asked about the location of my errant husband, I would give them a sad glance, look down, slowly twirl the ring on my finger, and not answer. They began to assume that I was a widow. This they understood. A widow was welcome. I thought I was safe, but then they said, "So, you must live with your son and his family. Where is he? When is he joining you?"

The Cost of Interaction

Organizers preparing
For a meeting yet to come
Already deep in conversation
Invited to join
I listened for a few moments
When they asked my opinion

The focus
A new program
Sex workers
Prostitutes
Some out of the business
Most still in
Choice, caste, or coercion
Each her own story to tell

And now
Attempting
To learn new skills
A different way
To live
Change the path
For those who would come next

A single issue
On the table
Child care
Should they provide
Child care
Such a simple question
Burdened by layers of reality
The shadows of
Working with people's lives
Where clear, clean lines do not exist

Provide a place
Where children would be safe
And fed
Where they would not be forced to see
What a child should never see
Silencing whispers
Of opium dripped
Into tiny mouths
So they sleep

Silent, hidden
Beneath the beds
Their mothers work upon.

But this choice
To provide a place of safety
While seeming so obvious
Has a downside
For if chosen it
Means the women
Are free
Free
To take more clients
To service more men

Again my opinion asked
Aware—a desire to hide
To avoid this cost of interaction
The messiness
The considered or imagined
Hide in ignorance
No training to guide this choice
And this was true
But even I knew
Training does not mean a crystal ball
And so I chose to speak
Words born from heart

Children
The most vulnerable
Deserve protection
Open the center
Work with the women
To offer a different way.
All the while know
Even the best intentions
Cannot predict which way
The winds will blow.

Others arrived
The start of the scheduled meeting
On to an agenda of
Numbers and facts
Budgets and reports to prepare
Safely within the world of black and white
While lives swirl amidst the grey.

We've Come a Long Way Baby!

I STILL CRINGE A LITTLE WHEN I THINK ABOUT THE first items the Anoothi women made. We started with semi-precious jewelry. With each craft fair and market, I prayed that the jewelry wouldn't break. Starting from zero was a steep learning curve. That first year was much more about selling the Anoothi story, not the value of the product. One person even said buying the product was a pity vote. That wasn't where any of us wanted to be.

Thankfully, we were willing to learn. We realized fairly quickly that making semi-precious necklaces didn't give the women a lasting skill and didn't honor their heritage. Over the years, we tried many different things. Some worked, some didn't. After much trial and error, we decided to look at revitalizing some of the traditional handicrafts of India. We ultimately focused on Kantha and hand-block printing.

The Kantha tradition takes recycled saris and essentially quilts them, often seven layers thick. The layers are held together by intricate and tiny, straight-line hand-stitching. These lines of stitching are only millimeters apart and create fabulous designs. The end result can be anything from a winter-ready bedspread to a lightweight shawl.

The women were constantly trying new designs. Whenever Jaimala and Hitesh visited Denver, they would come with loads of samples for me to curate. Some were instant winners—others not so much.

An example from their last trip:

We had settled down, ready to work. Anoothi samples were everywhere. My eyes landed on a piece of fabric, rolled tightly. It was about the shape and size of an army bedroll but, as with everything Indian, much more colorful. One side was a brilliant purple dotted with orange stitching. Unrolling it, I discovered the other side was a gorgeous floral print highlighted by purple vines and orange, red, and yellow flowers resembling our hibiscus.

This was the new Kantha yoga mat. It was obvious that it was a yoga mat but what was equally obvious, to my eyes, was how huge it was. Jaimala didn't believe me when I started talking about its size so I went upstairs and grabbed my own yoga mat from the closet. I quickly wiped the dust off and took it downstairs. We laid my mat on top of theirs, and saw that the Indian version was almost a foot wider and two feet longer.

The debate began! Perhaps the Indian version was better? But I described how crowded most yoga studios were and how these mats would take up too much room. We also learned there was a bigger problem. When we moved the mat from the carpeted floor of my basement to a tiled floor upstairs, trying to mimic the wood floor of a yoga studio, it became clear that the fabric was slippery, and didn't stick like the American versions with their rubbery grip. There was no way this could work. Beautiful as they were, they would be dangerous to work on. Downward Dog would become Frantic Faceplant. Jaimala and Hitesh would have to take the sample back to India, change the size, and decide if there was some way to put a backing on the fabric that wouldn't drastically change the price point.

We were all disappointed because the mats were stunning. Jaimala has one consistent reaction to disappointment—actually, to all emotions: a steaming cup of chai. During the visit, and for every visit, she was the official chai wallah. Don't think for one minute this includes using prepackaged American Chai spices. She would rather die! Each visit included a magical bag of Indian spices for food and a separate bag of her special Chai Masala.

Fifteen minutes later, disappointment soothed and thirst satiated, it was time to get back to work.

Invisible

8000 miles away
And farther from anything
I know as normal
Sounds, smells, sights
A camel with a red pom-pom on his nose
Sits by the side of the road
A blur of chaos
Barely held in check.

Days pass in a strange withdrawal
From cellphones and computers
As I lean into
Time spent teaching
Help the Aunties
Bathe the kids

Get them to bed
Calm the night terrors
That call out in the darkest hours
Play endless games
Push them higher and higher on swings
Simply in the moment and in the laughter.

And yet I am aware
A whisper of discontent
I try burying deep
In this village of cast-offs and orphans
What of mine is possibly big enough to mention
As I picture
The child next to me
Having had to beg
For a scrap of food.

Each day
Each challenge
I tell myself
It's not about me
This experience
It's about the kids
Being open
Learning, loving
It's not about me
And yet, I carried me along
Packed neatly in the growing pages of my journal

I promise
I'm not being the ugly American
I love the food
The spice, the freshness,
My fingers being the only utensil
Learning how to get food to my mouth
Proud when I'm told
I eat like an Indian.

I manage the temperatures
That swing from mind-numbing heat
To science experiments dissecting
Stems of plants to analyze
What happens when they freeze
Thankful for the layers I could pile on
That day everything froze
No worry how I look
In this place where lack of air conditioning or heat
Removes any concern for fashion.

I learn my bones can settle into the hard places
As nightly, plywood and wisps of cotton
Become the holders of my dreams
And soon, entire nights pass in full
Without the need to rise
Freezing temperatures
A short walk
To a bathroom that's a hole in the floor

Quickly redefine my needs.
I surrender to the inevitability of embarrassment
With frequent opportunities to practice
This resolve.
Take the women who come close to me
Staring
Poke the veins in my hand
Wonder why they stick out
And laugh saying loudly
"Your hands—they are ugly"

I feel the stigma of the minority
On the local bus
The only white face
The lone female
An uncommon language
Prevents me from
Bridging the gap
Watching the stares
Feeling the judgment
And yet, even so,
I have never felt so present in the journey.

But in the midst
As I celebrate each new experience
And pat myself on the back
For coping so well
I also shrink inside

Swallowed by the immensity
Of this land
Where so few know my name
Or care to know my story
Not a callousness on their part
But a reality
My story holds no relevance
In their lives

In the midst of inwardly chanting
It's not about me
It was all about me
 And it wasn't about me
A paradox as endless as the Indian sky.

The Nature of Intimacy

How do you define intimacy?
The sharing of secrets
Allowing deepest vulnerabilities to be seen
Sitting in easy silence
Or the communion of tears
Leaping forward to finish each other's sentences
Knowing the thought before it finds voice
Disagreeing deeply but still welcomed.

This friend of mine
We share those things
At least most of the time
At times, movement hard won
Involving a stretching
A give and take

We've both had to learn
So different
Color, culture,
Religion, upbringing
Yet connected
Determined to find
Common ground through it all.

This last trip
A new definition of intimacy
The conversation went a bit like this:

So when you visit America, what bothers you most?
For the most part I like America, you're too inde-
pendent, but I like America.
So nothing bothers you?
I didn't say that.
So what bothers you?
You really want to know?
Yes!
It's that whole tissue thing.

Now tissue for me means Kleenex
I am scrambling to decide
Do we blow our noses too loudly?
When she says

I mean you never really get clean.
Wait! You are talking about the bathroom?

Quickly I'm thinking, okay,
She's talking about toilet paper
Indians don't use toilet paper.
They use water and, well, their hand—

Yes, you never really get clean.
But your way—you are always wet.
At least we're clean!
But you're always wet and that's gross!!
Better to be clean and wet than dry and dirty!!!
It doesn't feel that way and really, with your new toi-
lets, you have that sprayer hose.
How about a switch to give a burst of air for instant
dryness?
You guys invented chess after all. A little dryer
shouldn't be hard.

A few snorts bubble from her nose
This seems a good sign
Then she says

At least we are clean.

Perhaps the snorts reflect being appalled
Rather than humorous agreement

As always she gets the last word
It's hard to continue after someone snorts
I am left dry
But with a fresh sense of intimacy.

The Men of Anoothi

JAIMALA AND HITESH VISITED DENVER AND STAYED with me for ten event-filled days. They were mid-way through their trip around the United States giving presentations and having meet-and-greets. These meetings were to educate people about Vatsalya's work in India, gain support, and obtain additional funding. Along with luggage holding their clothes and necessities, they brought an extra-large suitcase and a duffle bag full of Anoothi products. I couldn't wait to rummage through the bags and see items I had ordered for upcoming markets, and also to examine the samples that had been created since my last visit. After letting Jaimala and Hitesh get a good night's sleep, the first thing we did was spread all the items out on the floor of my office, down in the basement.

Looking through the samples I saw some lovely wooden animals about three inches tall—intricate, fanciful, yet oddly realistic. They were enchanting. I asked about them and learned that they were hand-carved, hand-painted, and that the artisans were men.

Men. This surprised me. Anoothi India, like Anoothi US, exists to empower women and historically has only worked with women. However, this group of male carvers had heard about Anoothi and how fairly the artisans were treated and paid. They wanted a similar opportunity and arranged a meeting with Jaimala and Hitesh. I was not involved in meetings like this as I had pulled away from daily business decisions for Anoothi India to concentrate on growing Anoothi US. After long discussions, Anoothi India decided to work with the men. This decision came from some deeply held beliefs: women are not empowered in the absence of men and all people deserve to be seen and valued regardless of gender. These men deserved the same respect being shown the Anoothi women.

As I listened to the story, I was impressed by the willingness of Anoothi India to grow and be flexible—to question in each circumstance "What is the best answer?" then move forward confidently in that direction. I was in total agreement with their decision and immediately placed an order for the animals. They would prove to be a consistent seller. These lovely animals brought needed revenue to the men, paid them a fair wage, and increased the profitability of Anoothi India, which benefited the women. Truly a win-win situation.

A year later, when I began to firm up the agenda for my upcoming return to India, I told Jaimala that I wanted to meet the men. There was a threefold purpose to this request. First, I wanted to see them at work and watch the process of how those amazing animals were created. Second, I wanted to talk with them and see if they would be willing to train some women in the craft. I was under the assumption that wood carving was a gender-prescribed role. I was hoping the increase in revenue from my orders might help them consider changing that tradition, possibly even making that a condition of my orders. Third, I wanted to talk with them about a new product possibility. Several times during holiday fairs, people saw their camels and asked if I had a Nativity set, a crèche. I was fascinated with the possibility of these gifted woodworkers creating a unique version of the Nativity scene.

Once I arrived in India, Jaimala told me she was working on setting up a meeting, but it was a touchy situation. The men wanted to meet with me, but it needed to be in secret. They sold in the government-sponsored tourist bazaars and couldn't afford to jeopardize those opportunities. If the government learned they were selling to an American, they could lose the contract. Even though it only paid the equivalent of pennies on the dollar, it was income they depended on.

As Jaimala continued to explore ways to meet, I began to search the internet for pictures that would help them understand the Nativity scene. I came across a good picture of the three Wise Men on camels and a few different depictions of the Nativity tableau. I also began the process of talking through the Christmas story with Jaimala, as she would need to explain the story and why, for example, there was a baby in a manger. She needed to be able to identify all the required players.

One Saturday night, a few days before I was scheduled to go back to the States, Jaimala and I were at Vatsalya. I was staying with her in her room. It was close to 11 p.m. and we were getting ready for bed when the phone rang. The meeting was set...for that night! We would meet the men at midnight. And so the journey began. Jaimala called one of the male staff on site to come and be our driver. While Jaimala was an excellent driver, it was evident there was a concern for our safety going off alone. A few minutes later we were off: Jaimala and I in the back, as was customary, while Ravisharan drove.

We rode in silence for about 15 minutes and then turned off the main road. Ravisharan began to drive into one of the villages. Suddenly we stopped and a man jumped into the passenger seat. As soon as the car door slammed, Ravisharan immediately sped off. Jaimala explained this was her contact with the artisans. His name was Aadesh and he was dressed in a full suit and tie as if going to any normal business meeting.

We spent the next hour traveling along meandering, bumpy dirt roads, going deeper into the desert. I had a few moments wondering what we were getting ourselves into and found myself grateful for the presence of Jaimala and our two male escorts. Suddenly Ravisharan and Aadesh begin talking rapidly. Ahead I saw a spot of light in the road. It was a man with a flashlight signaling for us to turn left onto a narrower road. A little further up was another man, another flashlight, and an even narrower road. This last signal took us into what was clearly some type of rural community, five dwellings huddled together surrounded by fields. More substantial than what I had seen in the slums, but clearly not affluent.

We were greeted by several men and a growing crowd of children. The kids were shy but curious. We went into one of the houses. We walked through an entryway and entered a room, perhaps the size of my American dining room, empty of all furniture other than four plastic chairs lined up against the wall—obviously put there just for us. The room was lit by lantern. At the far end a man sat on a small rug, working on carving and sanding elephants. He was wrapped in shawls and a head scarf because of the cold night air and completely focused on his work. He didn't even look up when we entered. I felt a sense of privilege being permitted to watch. There was complete silence as I began to take photos, but I realized that the room was filling with men, women, and children despite the late hour. After several moments, a woman came and took the man's place and began to work. Jaimala immediately started to ask questions about this and we learned that we had been mistaken. This work was not just being done by the men; the women were included! Such an exciting discovery to make.

While we were watching, Hanumant, the group's elder, entered the room. It's hard to describe how Indians revere their elders. It goes beyond politeness and respect. It permeates every action as it did that evening with Hanumant. Without knowing who he was, I knew exactly what position he held. This was his work, his legacy. They brought a chair for him to sit on and set it in the center of the room directly across from us. Everyone else remained standing on the cold concrete floor. Hanumant shared their collective story. He had three adult sons and his brother had five. All of these families, men and women, were involved in the woodworking. Decades of history doing this one type of carving. Oh my gosh! A clan. I realized for the first time I had the opportunity to work with a clan.

At this point, there were perhaps 30 or 40 people in the room. I often find myself overwhelmed in a crowd, particularly in a foreign place. This room was not large but there was something very, very different about this experience. I felt entirely comfortable and welcome. I could easily have been in a room with just five people.

After sharing some pleasantries, Jaimala took a moment to explain the request I was making. Then she began to tell the Christian Christmas story and Hindi words floated in the air. I recognized *Bhagwan* (God,) *bacha* (child,) *tin raja* (three kings,) and *unt* (camel,) but the language quickly eclipsed my knowledge. I settled back to just watch and enjoy. The children started inching closer. The adults began to lean in. There wasn't a sound in the room other than Jaimala's mesmerizing voice. A gifted storyteller was at work.

I wondered what they were thinking as I looked around the room at this group of Hindus, most of whom, if not all, were illiterate and had probably never encountered the Christmas story. A few seemed to nod when she mentioned Jesus as if they were aware of the name. Were they listening at multiple levels? Beyond the need to understand the characters in order to try and build the crèche? Were they comparing Hindu mythology to Christian mythology, or were they simply enjoying a good story?

I showed them the picture of the three Wise Men arriving on camels. Suddenly there was excitement in the room. This could be done. How tall did I want the final figures to be? Did I want realistic faces or more of an abstract presentation? Did I want goats and donkeys in the scene? I secretly hoped that someone would suggest an elephant. I'm not sure if that's in any version of the Nativity scene, but if it was being crafted by Indian artisans, it made a great deal of sense to me—and how cool would a kneeling elephant be?

After the story was finished and all the many questions answered, Jaimala turned to the young children, who by now had all migrated to a group at the front. She asked each of them their name. Never passing up an opportunity to validate the worth of a child, she took care to use the formal version of "you" and "your" rather than the Hindi informal. Soon a young girl stood up and began to sing a song. She sang with complete composure, owning her voice and the room. A younger boy then stood up and struggled to find that composure. I listened to what were clearly encouraging comments from several of the adults in the room when he finished singing.

Jaimala took one last moment to teach the children a portion of a song. She would sing a line and they would repeat it. Some of the adults nodded their heads in recognition. When I asked her what the song was about, she said it compared a child to a flower, unique and valued.

It was time for us to leave this magical evening. As we drove back to Vatsalya I was so quiet in the car that Jaimala asked if I was okay. Was I disappointed in some way? "Oh no," I said, "Hands-down, this was one of my all-time favorite experiences across all my trips to India. I was just wondering: can I adopt an entire clan?"

The Children

Part One—Alisha

An 8-year-old child
Beaten and broken
By the man meant
To build and shape
She moved slowly
Head down
Sadness etched on
A face that never smiled
Back of hand
Pressed against mouth
As if to remind
Never to smile
Never to speak.

Each trip
I took time to watch
She grew in size and spirit
Moments, still rare,
But moments
Of play and laughter
Of ease
The forgetting
What was before
The healing into
What was now
And should always
Have been.

Four years away
I wander
A new school
Courtyard full of children
Lessons held outside
Warmed by the soft winter sun.
Disoriented
So many new children
Or have they simply grown
And I don't recognize
The child, once small,
Now hidden in new-found-height
A face here and there
Yes, I know her, him

A few find me as well
And then, a voice,
"Delta Didi"
Standing in a doorway
Almost in shadow
A beautiful young woman
I don't know her
My brain reaches to remember
In the space of my pause
She is in my arms
Embracing me
"Welcome back, Delta Didi"

I know this voice but not this face
Stunned into silence
I see eyes twinkling with excitement
A smile that reaches beyond her face
And dances in the air
Strong, tall, confident
She now teaches those
Once like her
Her waist-length hair sways
With an air of casual elegance
Such is her beauty
Village families have reached out
To describe sons
Of marrying age
Such is her strength

She has said no
She will choose
Or not at all.

Miracles may happen
In that Hollywood flash
But most
Meander a longer route
Filled with ordinary moments
And extraordinary love
Until the wounding
Unravels
Loses presence and power
A faded color
Adding depth to the background
Of a truer story she calls her own.

The Children

Part Two—Abhik and Ameet

THEY WERE ALMOST FOUR YEARS OLD WHEN I FIRST met them. Two adorable boys, Abhik and Ameet, identical twins. One had an earring. This seemed out of place. I didn't see any other child with earrings, let alone a single earring. As with all things at Vatsalya, there was a story behind this. A year prior Abhik became ill and needed to be given medicine. The Aunties were afraid they would give the medicine to the wrong boy. At Vatsalya, ingenuity reigns and an answer was quickly found. Little Abhik had one ear pierced, was given the correct medicine, the Aunties were happy, and all was well with the world.

Scamps. Little scamps—that is the best word to describe those two. On my first volunteer trip to Vatsalya, I spent three months teaching in the nursery, which is the equivalent of pre-K and kindergarten, so I had quite a bit of time to get to know Abhik and Ameet as we learned Hindi and English together. You could just see the mischief brimming in their eyes. Like most twins, they were joined at the hip. I almost never saw one without the other.

First thing in the morning, they would greet me on the way to breakfast and I would pick them both up and twirl around in circles. We would laugh and laugh. But then, something happened—

That first trip
So magical
Yet, difficult
In unexpected ways
Only a few weeks in
I needed a moment
To myself
Skipping lunch
I decided to bathe
Coming back
To my unit
Wet flip flops
Concrete
I fell
A hard fall
Slipping seven concrete steps
Landing
At the bottom
On my back

Feeling the crease
Of two stairs
Cutting into
My hip
And the middle of my back
Staring
At the Indian sky
Wondering
If my trip had just ended.

After the breath
Returned
The pain joined
And I knew I was hurt
But hoped
Nothing broken
Only one thing to do
Move
Everyone would
Be gone for at least an hour
And I could not stay there
For an hour.

So I rolled over,
Gingerly crawled
Up the steps
And forced
Myself to stand

Perhaps it wasn't
So bad after all
Everything moved
Everything worked
If I moved slowly enough.

I walked to Jaimala's office
Forgetting
She was not there
She had returned to Jaipur
Feeling foolish and small
I told the staff I needed to talk
With her.

I called and could tell
My call was a bit of an irritation
She was supposed to be helping
Children, not dealing with silly volunteers
Or perhaps that was just my fear
Speaking loudly in my head.

She told me the jeep
Would bring me to
Her brother-in-law,
The Doctor,
He would know what needed to be done

The jeep was already packed
With children and items
That needed to be transported
They found room for me
In the back
I hid under a shawl
Holding my knees
And cried silent tears
As every bump
Traversed my body.

At the house
Jaimala asked
If she could look at my back
Already a bruise,
A vicious combination
Of purple and black
Spread the size
Of a baseball glove
Across my lower back
And hip

Within the hour
I was at the hospital
Queues disappeared when
The Doctor's name
Was invoked
Many tests and hours

Later
I was sent home
Pain pills,
A pain spray,
And admonished
To lie flat
For at least a week
In order to heal.

India,
I had come to India
To serve
To be of service
And now
I was lying
In the medical unit
On the campus
Watching geckos
Race across the ceiling
I found myself
Disappearing into
A mass of self-pity.

Jaimala gently chided
She said, the children
Have no need of your service
They are fine whether you are here
Or back in your country.

But they can benefit
Greatly from your love
From your interest in their lives
As you can benefit from their
Interest in yours.
This can still happen
Heal
And then
There will still be time
To be with the children.

I wish I could list
All of the lessons
This woman
This place
These children
Taught me

And, of course,
As always
She was right
I healed
Enough, though stiff
And slow,
To move back
Into the unit
With the older girls.

The first morning back
As the sun was starting to wake
There came a knocking at the door
And young voices
"Delta Didi, Delta Didi"
I rose
Blanket trailing behind
And made my way to the door
Opening, I saw the grinning faces
Of Ameet and Abhik.
Normally I would have
Picked them both up and
Twirled our magic circle game
But I could not
Not yet
Intuitively they understood
Each took a hand
Walked me
To a concrete bench
And both climbed
Up onto the bench
And leaned
One on my right
One on my left
Nestled into my sides
Heads resting on my shoulders
We stood
And watched the sunrise.

Coming back years later, I wonder: Will they remember me? Will I recognize them? They are almost 10 now. As I wander the beautiful campus, a young lad approaches me, holds out his hand and says, "Namaste, Delta Didi." Instantly, I realize that it is one of the twins, but I have no idea which one. I see that he doesn't have an earring and so I say, "Namaste, Ameet." The grin captures his entire face and I feel the warmth spread into my heart. I later learn that I guessed well, as Abhik no longer has an earring either!

As they have grown, they have developed slight differences. Ameet is a little taller and Abhik sports a small scar on his forehead. After spending a few moments with me, Ameet runs off to play cricket with his friends. I see Abhik across the campus, playing with a different group of friends. Their confidence has grown and they no longer rely solely on each other for friendship and support. Before long, Abhik sees me and comes up and greets me. It is clear they both remember me. It is also clear that playing with friends is much more important than hanging around with an adult who doesn't speak Hindi—and this is just as it should be.

The Children

Part Three—Sitara

Sitara, and
Two younger sisters
Came

Their mother
A prostitute
Who didn't seem
To care

And yet
Cared enough
To send them away.

Ah, this girl. She never stopped smiling or laughing,
bringing a sense of joy to everything and everyone. I had

sponsored Sitara and spent more time with her than the other children. We would walk around the campus and she would hold my hand. During dance nights, she would grab me from the crowd of adults comfortably watching and insist that I dance. She didn't care that I didn't know any of the Bollywood dance moves. She just wanted me to be having as much fun as she was having. She was easy to love.

Months later, I learned the girls had returned to their family home. I wondered what Sitara's life would be like. Her family was conservative Muslim, but Vatsalya was an ecumenical, progressive campus where she had been taught independence and to speak for herself. This self-reliance was uncommon in the villages and would not necessarily be valued or understood. Would she continue her education on her own? How would a future husband react to her independent spirit? I wondered if I would ever see her again.

Imagine my surprise when, shortly before my next trip to India, Jaimala notified me that she had hired Sitara to work at Vatsalya as the events coordinator. When I arrived on campus, her smiling face was one of the first that I saw and it was as if no time had passed. We were both a little older but that was all. She still seemed to live each moment with complete joy. She told me that she had continued her education, going to college. Such an amazing feat!

I was at Vatsalya on National Republic Day and witnessed Sitara at work. She had created an entire program that the children presented and it was done flawlessly. As

I sat through the program, I found myself thinking about what Sitara's life would have been like if her mother hadn't sent her to Vatsalya. Would she have followed her mother into the sex trade? Possibly—probably. But instead, through her strength of will and the never-ending support of Vatsalya, this is one of many examples where the cycle seems to have been broken.

A Postscript

India is not for the faint of heart. Jaimala wrote me that Sitara had left Vatsalya. She was to be married. Her mother had arranged a marriage with an unemployed, illiterate young man from their village. Jaimala tried to convince her to stay, but Sitara felt she must do as her mother asked. But she told Chhoti Maa (the children's name for Jaimala), "Don't worry. I am happy. I am always happy."

Many years ago, I had given Jaimala some money to set aside for a wedding gift for Sitara, when and if the time came. In her letter, Jaimala asked if she could keep that money for a future time instead of giving it to Sitara for the wedding. She had a sense that there would come a time when Sitara would need that money. Jaimala's intuitive sense of those in her care has never failed and so I immediately said yes.

It is easy to be sad about Sitara's choice and to think "what a waste of such a bright, beautiful soul." But there is something about this girl. If there is anyone who can come out on top still with a smile on her face, it's Sitara.

The Children

Part Four—Preeti

Her story
She arrived
Only five years old
On the streets for over a year
Parents who knew
    Only how to drink
           And to swing a fist
So she ran away
Three years old, she ran away
           And began to beg.

    Wait, wait, wait. My brain cannot process this. Through my American lens, it is not possible that a three-year-old child runs away. How is this even a thought, let *alone a possibility? I understand wandering away, following a blowing flower, or seeing a sparkly bauble. But consciously choosing to run away. Three years old??? No, NO, **NO**!*

And yet, this is not America. This is India, where she not only ran away, but found ways to survive.

A baba, old and weathered
 Took her in
  Promised shelter and food
   Exchanged for what he called games
    Which surely meant
     Or so he said
      That she was loved.

Until a kindly priest, from a local temple, brought her to Vatsalya. She began to live in the unit for the younger girls. The Aunties helped her to learn the daily routine—helped her understand she didn't have to hide food. There would be enough to eat.

But trauma is deep
 Not easily relieved
  She simply wanted
   To play the games
    She had learned

> That involved touching
>   And could not understand
>   Why others were afraid
>   After all,
>   This was love.

Years of therapy combining the best of East and West
A counselor
    To unravel the complicated thoughts and fears
Yoga and massage
    To remind the power of breath and reshape the
    power of touch
A small rabbit
    To care, to tend, to love
An older child as mentor
    To provide the possibility of friendship
But through it all, nothing seemed to change and other
children became more afraid of her as she grew older.

Over the years it seemed that nothing was working. Preeti continued to act out, sometimes in ways that seemed dangerous to herself or the other children. She continued to fail academically. There were continual discussions among the staff. Vatsalya sought guidance from a global council they had convened for just such purposes. It was finally decided to let her leave school and begin helping the Aunties. It was a solution of sorts, it kept Preeti supervised and everyone safe, but it still felt incomplete.

A few years back, I remember asking Jaimala what would happen to Preeti after she turned 18, as Vatsalya is only equipped to care for children until that age. Jaimala paused for quite some time and then responded, "While I don't know what will happen, it is likely that she will find a man and marry and in all likelihood the man will not treat her well." It was my turn to be silent, as this response felt like truth but weighed heavily in the air. I asked Jaimala how she coped with realities like that. Again, she was silent for many moments and then responded, "I cannot take care of the future. What I can do, for Preeti and for each of the children in my care, is love them while they are with me. I love them totally and fully. They know they are cared for. They know they are respected. They know they are loved. This I can do."

Until you experience it, you cannot fathom the power of that love. I have heard the phrase unconditional love all my life. I have witnessed it only in one place: Vatsalya.

Four Years Later

Fast forward four years. I return to Vatsalya and discover that Preeti is still there. She has become the official tour guide and a language liaison for English speakers. Without anyone knowing it, Preeti had developed quite a talent with English. She now greets everyone who comes to the campus and escorts them around explaining the history, pointing out the computer lab, vocational units, the organic fields that produce a large percentage of the food consumed at Vatsalya, and so on. Because of this job, she can stay at Vatsalya.

A place where she can be whole.

The Children—Epilogue

Alisha, Abhik and Ameet, Sitara, and Preeti. Children that have all come from places of trauma with completely different stories. Five children who bear witness to the ability of love and security to transform lives.

Anywhere between 50 and 75 children live at Vatsalya at any given time. Imagine if I could tell you all of their stories.

To Be Seen

Two days of training
Day one went well
The second so different
Her eye black and bleak
The other women
Acted as if
Nothing was wrong
And perhaps it wasn't
Perhaps this was
Normal for her life
And theirs
Spread through
Assorted days.

I had no language

To reach out

And tell her

Of another way

And so

The work continued

All around

I chose to sit across

Hold her firmly in my gaze

Hoping she would understand

That she would know

She was seen

She was

Worth

Being seen

Even as

I worried

There should be more

I could do.

Inside Out

Angry
I find myself angry
That's too strong
Irritated
Like an eye twitching
Or the smallest pebble
Hidden between toes
I am irritated
Four years away
Four years and
Still
There are
Men urinating
Peeing for God's sake
On street corners

Even in cities
Where they are educated
They
They
How did I shift
Into language
Of they and them
The land of the other
Where judgement licks
Ugly lips waiting
In eager anticipation
To scan the outer landscape
And identify flaw and failure
In the finest detail.

How have I come to this small place
Where eyes
Magnify wrong, not right
Everywhere I look
Trash
On the footpaths
The roads
In front of every shop
Even the park
The beautiful park
With the winding paths
And glorious flowers
I watch a couple

Share a picnic lunch
Then throw their trash
On the grass
Walk to their car
Which is clean and new
Screaming of the wealth
Sweeping these cities
And drive away
They should know better
The pebble in my shoe
Has grown into a boulder.

Even this event
Anticipated eagerly
Movie night at the house
Snacks made
Each person
A chosen spot
Opening credits roll
So loud
Everything, everyone
So loud
The noise
Rumbles the speakers
I watch
Them
Amazed at what is normal
And causes no discomfort

But I swirl
Rocked by frantic commotion
Leaving only
A desire to wrap myself
In soft cotton
And pull away
To shut them out
No still center
Where I can rest.

The season is different
Far from what I've known before
Cold and wet
A bleak winter
That greys the exterior
And shrinks my interior
The final straw
Hard rain
In a tuk-tuk
Bitter wind
Unavoidable pothole
My head cracked against the metal frame
Soaked from the splash
My soul is drowning.

The First Taste Belongs to the Gods

So changed this time
Juggling the question
Why
The magic gone
The honeymoon
Run over
Smashing glasses
Once rose colored
Plus enough time
Enough trips
I shouldn't have to try so hard
Surely they could meet me halfway.

Each day tired and heavy
I wake, not bursting with ideas,
But wishing
Already
For the day to be over
So I can come back
To my bed
But even then
Peace eludes
As I stare at darkness
Not counting sheep
But asking why
My thoughts are living here
This space so devoid of grace
And as I judge them

I judge myself
The audacity of my thoughts
Shames me
Time and again I whisper
Be grateful
Thankful for the opportunity
Grateful to learn
And all of this I know
But it does little to silence
The voice screaming inside.

I don't know how to shift this gaze
And with nothing left to do
At last, I choose
To let go
The thoughts will be what they will be
Give them room to roam
As each new thought comes about
I stop, trying to discern
Truth from drama
Calling upon tools learned
Is it true?
Stopping to ask
Is it always so?
Yes, men still pee in the streets
But not all men
Not on every street
Not on this street

At least not that I've seen
And somehow this makes me smile.
Over and over
Each thought massaged
Until the tightness begins to melt
And I settle softer at night
A new rhythm hesitantly emerges
Lacking finesse but
More in sync with those around
The trip will end too soon
To resolve all that has been disturbed
And the honeymoon
Has indeed ended
But I am left with the thought
That I have left the land
Of they and them
To enter a new place
Sometimes brittle and stark
But oh, if I am willing
To clean my mirror
And look with clear eyes
Both within and without,
There is the hope
The truest chance
I can meet you
Simply being who I am.

Mistakes

IT'S IMPOSSIBLE TO TRAVEL TO NEW PLACES, NEW CUL-
tures, and not make mistakes. In the years of going back
and forth to India, I have made several. Particularly in the
early years, I was always on guard, trying to make sure that
I didn't do anything to offend my Indian colleagues or to
come off as the intolerant American.

But back to mistakes. Sometimes I don't even know
they have been made. As an example, I'd returned to India
after a few years away. It was my first day back on the campus and I was eagerly catching up with staff and children
after being away for so long. I went into the kitchen. What
is it about kitchens? They are always the center of activities and gossip. I walked in and saw Aaradhya, one of the
Aunties. She is probably five feet tall. However, don't mistake her small size for meekness.

She saw me and smiled. I knew better than to walk over and hug her. Like most Indians, she's not one for public displays of affection. The smile was her hug. There were several staff and volunteers in the kitchen. I was quickly introduced to those I didn't know. Ravisharan was in the kitchen. He has been at Vatsalya all the years I have been coming, as has Aaradhya. One of the new staff tried to introduce me to him and two things happened simultaneously. I began to say that I already knew him and Aaradhya began talking loudly and quite pointedly. It's always amazing to me that I don't have to understand Hindi to understand at least the feel of what is being said. And this time it was clear that Aaradhya was upset—very upset! I kept hearing Ravisharan's name. He was staring at the floor and the look on his face clearly said that he wished he was somewhere else. Suddenly I was hearing my name as well. The group in the kitchen was looking back and forth between Ravisharan and me like a critical tennis match was going on. I had no idea what was being said. I heard the word Pushkar and realized Aaradhya was saying something about a trip we had taken with the children a few years before.

The Colonel, a friend of Jaimala's, owned a resort in the town of Pushkar. Each year Pushkar is inundated with nomads and herders as the site of one of India's largest camel fairs. The fair coincides with a sacred holiday and pilgrims come from around the world to bathe in the holy lake of Pushkar Sarovar. The Colonel invited Jaimala to bring some of the children to his resort around the time of the camel fair. Twenty-one children and five staff members, including me, were soon on a bus on our way to Pushkar. Apparently, I had been promoted from volunteer to honorary staff member.

The bus left early and the children were all wrapped in shawls to guard against the cold air. They also each carried a brown paper bag. I started to ask another staff member what that was for but got distracted by an elephant in the road. After about 45 minutes on the road, I noticed that many of the bus windows were being lowered. This surprised me because it was quite cold outside. The next thing I knew several of the kids were throwing up—hence the need for the brown paper bags. The children of Vatsalya are rarely in vehicles for any extended length of time. As a result, many of them suffer from fairly extreme motion sickness in cars or buses. All I will say is it made the trip quite long and smelly.

We finally arrived at the resort in Pushkar. It was lovely. Our host had set up five spacious tents for us. These were equipped with comfortable cots, electric lighting, rugs over the flooring, a water dispenser, and portable heaters. After the children and staff were distributed among the tents and our bags put away, we met in the gardens for a formal welcoming reception. We sat in a large circle and the Colonel welcomed us as his most honored guests and put a large garland of marigolds over each of our heads. He invited the children to sing and dance and they, always eager for an audience, instantly began performing. We spent a lovely hour or so in that circle, eating sweets, singing songs, and listening to birds chirp in the background.

The rest of the trip blurred with visits to the holy lake and the temple, admiring camels, and playing in the swimming pool that the Colonel had filled to a low level just for the children. None of them knew how to swim but this didn't stop any of them. Before long everyone, except Aaradhya was in the water playing racing games and anything else we could think of. Aaradhya watched from a distance safe enough to guarantee that water would not accidentally splash her. She had towels ready for each waterlogged child as they emerged. After two and a half days of festivities we were on the bus, with new brown paper bags, and headed back to Vatsalya.

This was my memory of Pushkar and the trip. I kept thinking about it as Aaradhya continued her harangue, which seemed to clearly focus on Ravisharan. Perhaps this was just wishful thinking on my part because I kept hearing my name as well. Finally, I couldn't stand it any longer and I interrupted her.

Auntie, Auntie, tell me what you are saying.

I looked at her while I said this but everyone knew that she doesn't speak English. An awkward silence filled the room.

At last, one of the senior staff members began to explain the reason Aaradhya was so upset. At the garland ceremony, Ravisharan and I sat next to each other and had garlands placed over our heads. It was as if we were a couple and promised to each other. For a minute, I was sure this was a joke. Seriously? I was easily thirty years older than he was. But as everyone averted their eyes when I scanned the room, and Ravisharan kept staring a hole in the floor, it was clear this had been a serious faux pas.

I was at a complete loss. I had no idea what to do or how to make this right, and clearly Ravisharan was in the same position. I did the only thing I knew to do. I walked over to Aaradhya, bent down and touched her feet, in a sign of respect, and said:

Auntie, I am so sorry. It was just a mistake. We meant no harm.

A staff member interpreted and again there was a long silence in the room. Finally, Aaradhya looked at me, gave me a big smile and nodded her head. I had the sense that I had been forgiven. She walked out of the kitchen without even glancing at Ravisharan. I think his forgiveness is going to take many more years.

India

WHEN PEOPLE LEARN THAT I HAVE BEEN TO INDIA THEY often ask, "Did you like it?" That is a hard question for me to answer. India is a difficult country that both soothes and assaults the senses. There is beauty and ugliness in every breath, in every view. For me, the challenge seems to be finding a way to acknowledge both. Being willing to see a beautiful woman, in her elegant, fine sari, next to a beggar who cannot walk and is using his hands to crawl up the stairs.

A second question usually follows the first, "What did you like most about India?" There is an easy answer to that—the people. They are warm, welcoming, and engaging. But I have always felt a need to look beyond that and determine what I really liked most about India itself. I finally know the answer.

Life in India dances between the secular and the sacred without missing a beat.

I think of being on a crowded street when suddenly everything stopped. I started to ask what was happening when I realized not only had movement stopped but everything was quiet and hushed—reverential. Coming down the street, dressed in white, was a procession of men, carrying a wrapped body above their heads—a Muslim funeral procession. There was no hearse, no coffin, at least not at this stage, no separation between the living and the dead.

In my early trips there was a guest room at the office. When I stayed in that room, I would awaken to a staff member unlocking the office doors. I could hear him moving from room to room, clearing the air with incense before placing a lighted stick in front of an altar.

I watched children clamoring to learn classical Indian dances that can be traced back to the earliest of sacred dances performed in ancient Hindu temples. But they remain alive and vital today.

I listened as Jaimala and the Vatsalya staff thoughtfully chose names for children that arrived at the home. They often arrived with derogatory nicknames, but at Vatsalya, each child received an honorable name. The names often come from Sanskrit, a liturgical language of Hinduism that dates back more than 4,000 years in parts of India.

So much of what I have learned has come through my friendship with Jaimala. She is a force of nature. She packs more into one day than most of us do in a week. I have never met someone who works harder or loves more fiercely. And yet, somehow, she keeps this delightful balance where play and rest are also part of her normal routine. She's quick to begin dancing or singing and we have equally passionate discussions about Anoothi, her love for Obama, or movies starring Tom Hanks. I'm not sure a day went by at Vatsalya when she wouldn't educate me about a certain Sanskrit phrase or explain the meaning of some tradition. In passing she would relate a story of Hanuman, the Monkey God, and then go back to teaching me how to use the washing machine at their house.

What do I like most about India? Movements, decisions, even the daily routines of life are formed through this wonderful intertwining of culture, history, religion, and philosophy. There is no separation. It is all just life in India.

The First Taste
Belongs to the Gods

I have yet to find
A place
Where you are ill-at-ease
But when I think
Of where you are most alive
Two images
Spin in delightful equilibrium
You sitting
Amidst a circle of grinning children
Or cooking in a kitchen
Fresh spices at your fingertips

I remember
The first time
You invited me

Into your kitchen
It felt such sacred domain
I was not invited to help
That would take longer
Instead I watched and listened
As you toasted cardamom and mustard seeds
And spun stories of life

You told me
The test
Your future mother-in-law
Age-old tradition
Cook a perfect chapatti
This despite
Your being Brahmin
The highest of high
Choosing to marry
Between castes
Choosing to marry
For love
Both choices so unusual

I can see you
Standing in front of the flame
Forming your dough into
The perfect-sized ball
Rolling it out
A flawless circle

The First Taste Belongs to the Gods

Slapping it onto the pan
Using the flame to brown
All under the watchful
And critical eyes
Of the woman
Into whose house
You would move.

Nervous is hard to imagine
Yet you talk of butterflies
Little trembles in your fingers
I ask how the chapatti turned out
And you simply smile
And say,
He's my husband, isn't he?

A few months later
I am back in your kitchen
This time invited to help
Simple tasks
Cut the tomatoes
Dice the onions
Even so, I'm careful
To ask about size and quantity
To make sure
It is perfect
I wonder why
I am being so cautious

Only to understand
That cooking here,
In this space
By your side
Feels like
Participating in art
Ritual and tradition
Gracing daily need
No recipes
Each dish handed down
From mother to daughter

You seem most the artist
When surrounded by spices
No bottled jars
Containing pre-ground cumin or ginger
It is here I learn
Turmeric and ginger come from a root
You smash with the heel of your hand
Against the countertop before using
No culinary tools
Beyond knives and a
Worn mortar and pestle

I learn to listen for the delightful sound
Of cardamom and cumin seeds popping
Removed from the heat
Just before burning

Nothing measured
Just used with knowledge
Found buried in your molecules
Gleaned through generations

Smelling pots of daal and vegetable sabzi
Bubbling on the stove
I realize
I've never seen you stop
Taste your cooking
A step of the process
I ask about this
And a rare flash of surprise
Crosses your flushed face
The spoon is set down
And you gaze fully at me
Eyes no longer twinkling
Now serious with intent
No,
A Hindu does not taste
While food is being prepared
It's simple, you see,
The first taste belongs to the Gods.

My experience of Jaimala is highlighted by moments like this. She will remain my friend and sister for the rest of my life. Of this I have no doubt. She has already told me so. (Remember what I said about who always gets the last word?)

There is much about India, its culture, its religion, its philosophy, that I have barely begun to understand. But this sentiment expressed by Jaimala in the kitchen, "The first taste belongs to the Gods,"—this I understand.

AND IT SEEMS, TO ME, TO BE A LOVELY WAY TO LIVE.